ABOVE MEXICO CITY

BY ROBERT CAMERON AND HERB LINGL

A new collection of original and historical
aerial photographs of Mexico City

Text by Luis Herrera-Lasso M.

CAMERON and COMPANY, San Francisco, California

Page 2: An impressive view of the city toward the east. In the background the Popocatépetl and Iztaccíhuatl volcanoes can be seen. At right is one side of the Aragón Forest where one of the city's two zoos is located.

Page 3: The Paseo de la Reforma was designed and built in the nineteenth century in the tradition of great French boulevards. Seen here from west to east, in the foreground is the Independence Column, by architect Antonio Rivas Mercado, built in 1910 to celebrate the centennial of Mexican independence. The downtown historical district is in the background at right, the Latin American Tower silhouetted on the skyline.

Page 4: In this panoramic view, taken from the Polanco area, the volcano Iztaccihuatl (17,380 feet) is visible in the background, to the east of the valley next to the volcano Popocatépetl (17,900 feet, at right surrounded in mist). The landscape seen from this perspective is the most characteristic profile of the valley of Mexico. The majority of the mountains surrounding the valley are covered by dense coniferous forest that begins to thin at 11,500 feet.

Page 5: The Popocatépetl volcano is the second highest point in all of Mexico, surpassed only by the Pico de Orizaba, 87 miles to the east, at 18,406 feet above sea level. The crater is threatening, above all since the mid nineties when it began moderate activity, periodically releasing puffs of smoke several kilometers high as well as incandescent rocks which can be seen falling from the cone at night.

Such a book as this does not reach publication without more than the usual cooperaion from many people. So, for their encouragement and expertise, we thank the following:
Anilu Aceves Aduana, Alejandro Aguilera, Clemente Q Mieles Alonso, Raquel Valverde Aranda, Axel Araño, Alicia Buenrostro, Anthony Cameron, Sebastian Robinson Carrion, Abigail Carvajal, Leonardo Mieles Cifuentes, Pedro Cote, Alfonso Cruz, Michael Calderwood, Jeffreys Corner, Marco Cortes, Adolfo Crespo y Vivo, Fernando Delmar, Alfonso de Maria, Robert Ekstrand, Richard Elliott, Don Flaten, Georgina Lagos Donde, Alfonso Flores, Norma Gales, Axel Garaño, John Goy, Hans Hoefer, Christian Hoenig, Linda Henry, Scott Henderson, Naomi Hirooka, Andres Hofmann, Markus Jebsen, Manuel Rivero Lascurain, Rafael Rivero Lascurain, Luis Adolfo Mendez Lugo, Angeles Mastretta, Lorena Migoya Mastretta, Gabriela Cesarman Maus, Terry McGerry, Jose Ariel Mendoza, Patricia Mendoza, Jill Merlin, Dan Norris, Antonio Ovando, Mary Petrin-Kehoe, Enrique Ayalu Rodriguez, Paola Carcia Romero, Enrique Ayalu Rodriguez, Gerardo Rojano, Scott S. Robinson, Isabelle Rosseau, Fernando Sandoval, Fidencio Ortiz San Juan, Stephanie Salter, Leobardo Sarabia, Zaidee Stavely, Arturo Samando Uribe, Catherine Valle, Marco Velazquez, Victor Velazquez, Fernando Valencia Villasenor and Angel Davila Zuleta.

Special mention goes to Robert E. Burger, Angel Demerutis Flores, Bernardo Mendez Lugo and Laura Gallart Ramos for devoting an exceptional amount of time and talent toward the making of this book.

Thanks to the following for providing historical photography: Archivos General de la Nacion, Mexicana Airlines and the National Aeronautics and Space Administration.

Color processing by The New Lab, San Francisco, Laboratorio Mexicano de Imagenes, Mexico City. Cameras by Pentax.

CAMERON and COMPANY

680 EIGHTH STREET, SUITE 205 SAN FRANCISCO, CA 94103 800 779 5582 www.abovebooks.com

Library of Congress Control Number: 2004109828
Above Mexico City ISBN 0-918684-66-8
© 2004 by Robert W. Cameron and Company, Inc. All rights reserved.

First printing, 2004.

Design: Toki Design, San Francisco
Printed in China

TABLE OF CONTENTS

INTRODUCTION

THE AERIAL PHOTOGRAPHY OF ROBERT CAMERON AND HERB LINGL is displayed at its best in the broad and beautiful expanse of Mexico City. Every aspect of this great metropolis here reveals its personality, and yet it can be seen all at once, as a whole.

Though a flight may take fifteen minutes from one side of the city to the other, such is the immediacy of these photographs by Cameron and Lingl that you can almost hear the church bells ringing at six o'clock, feel the rain on a summer afternoon, or bend to the wind in the trees of Chapultepec. If you happened to be outdoors in Mexico City while this collection of aerial photographs was being shot, your image would be here.

Half of the population of this city has come from elsewhere, bringing their individuality and aspirations with them. In only eight years, the city has grown from six to more than twenty million people, making this the largest in the world.

As school children we were taught that our city was built atop another one. We learned that the conquering Spaniards of the sixteenth century were surprised to find that Tenochtitlan, as it was called then, was as large as Rome at that time. Under the cathedral the Spaniards built was the temple Tialoc, and the routes that the Aztecs used to go to the temple are the same paths that now criss-cross the city.

In the same way we are surprised today to be able to view the magnificent scope as well as the intricate detail of this great city from above. Here the light of the sunset illuminates the reds and yellows of colonial architecture; showing the shapes of stones in pre-hispanic buildings; with a panoply of mirrors reflecting the silhouette of the city in the glass of modern skyscrapers.

With these photographs you can walk the city from an aerial perspective, from contemporary to baroque buildings, from the Palacio de Iturbide to the Arzopispado. The famous writer Salvador Novo, who chronicled Mexico City in the twentieth century, would surely have loved to walk with his cronies through these photographs. Perhaps only a nineteenth century artist, Jose Maria Velasco, anticipated this aerial perspective, when he chose to paint Mexico from a bird's eye view, framed in volcanoes.

But the modern artists who created this book have added the perspective of time, with historical photographs that lead you to the old city, the one connected by train to San Angel, Coyoacan, or Azcapotzalco, and further south to Xochimilio, to travel in a Chinampa through prehispanic eras. You can sense how deep this history is when you realize that in the time of Azcapotzalco shown here the population of the city was less than 450,000.

These unqiue aerial perspectives reveal clearly the contrast between the classic colonial style of architecture, which ended early in the last century, and the thrust of contemporary Merican design. At the four points of the compass the outskirts of the city come to life: On the south lie mountains that shield the city of "never ending spring," Cuernavaca. Due east, the magnificent colonial enclave Puebla is hidden behind the volcanoes Potocatepetl and Iztlacihuatl. To the north sleeps the astonishing, sacred tenth-century city Teotihuacan. And in the northeast is the ceremonial center Tula.

As I write this I marvel at how little I know of my own homeland thus I am inspired by this collection to compare the landmarks and the byways of this magnificent city to the great photographs of the past, by Charnay and Briquet, by the Mayo and the Casasola brothers, and by Mexico's eminent recent photographers such as Nacho Lopez and Hector Garcia. Now Robert Cameron and Herb Lingl have added a crowning visual achievement—from above.

—Luis Herrera-Lasso M.

CENTER

At night the main square, or Zócalo, glows at Christmas (left) and from a rising moon (right). The National Palace and the Santa Teresa dome bask under the moon. The latter neoclassical structure, a former church designed by Cristobal de Medina Vargas and built in 1678–1684, is now an art and performance center. It was converted to this use in the early 1990s by architect Luis Vincente Flores.

Opposite: The Zócalo represents religious and political themes, with the Cathedral at center and the National Palace at right. Built on top of the ruins of the ancient Aztec capital of Tenochtitlán, this plaza pulls together the different stages of Mexican history: the remains of the pre-Hispanic city's Templo Mayor, controversially restored in the 1980s (to the right of the Cathedral), to modern warehouses of the 1930s (foreground), flanking the southern entry to the plaza via 20 de Noviembre Avenue.

Two perspectives on the main square: at left a plaza between the cathedral and the Aztec temple, a culture gap; at right, the National palace and its gardens in a rare rear view. The latter is now mainly symbolic, as presidential headquarters are at 'Los Pinos' in Chapultepec Park. This building has been restored mostly as a museum and is devoted to ceremonial events.

The telecommunications giant Telmex stands out in the urban sprawl of the San Rafael neighborhood (foreground) with Cuauhtémoc in the background. On the left is the Railroad Hospital, in 1930s art deco style.

Opposite: A few blocks to the north of the Zócalo is the church of the former convent of Santo Domingo, one of the first buildings of the Spanish conquerors between 1527 and 1532. The current church was finished in 1736, once housed the Holy Inquisition. The expropriation of church properties in the Reform laws in the mid 19th century turned the area to street use and diminished the church's original look. In addition to the church, some cloisters have been preserved and integrated to house the National Education Library. At left, a modern structure covers a colonial patio.

The Pemex Tower of the 1970s, by architect Pedro Moctezuma, built during the oil rush of José Lopez Portillo's presidency, ranked as the tallest building in the city until the Torre Mayor. At right, the Tower with the Reforma skyline in the background, and at left, seen at sunset towards the eastern mountains.

The Monument to the Revolution, by architect
Carlos Obregón Santacilia, employed the
metallic structure designed for the central
vestibule of the Legislative Palace. The construction of this monumental building was
interrupted by lack of funds after the
Revolution of 1910.

Two panoramic views of the western zone of the historical district, in which the Alameda Park and the Palace of Fine Arts stand out. In the background at right is the Tlatelolco neighborhood, which constituted the northern border of the city in the 1940s, surpassed by the urban sprawl since the late 1950s.

Heavy traffic on Eje Central, seen from the Historical District towards the south. Right foreground, the Victoria building of the early 1990s by architects Alberto Kalach, Daniel Álvarez and Axel Arañó. Here are government offices and a metro station (San Juan de Letrán) arranged around a circular patio.

Opposite: The Alameda from the west: Left foreground, the annex of the 1970s National Lottery building, at the intersection of Juárez and Reforma Avenues, by architect David Muñoz. At center, the Sheraton Hotel, part of the restoration of the perimeter of the Alameda, hit hard by the 1985 earthquake.

Reforma Avenue in the western part of the city is the axis of the financial district and wealthy residential areas rooted in the late nineteenth century. On the left, in the background, are new developments west of the city, such as Santa Fe and Interlomas. On a very clear day, as in the photograph on the left, one can see the volcano Nevado de Toluca. Above the view is reversed, east to the historic center, with La Palma roundabout glorietta in the foreground.

Designed for the Centennial of the Independence in 1910 by architect Antonio Rivas Mercado, this column is crowned by a gold-leafed sculpture known as the Angel of Independence. The steps to the platform of this monument (not visible in the historical picture) are witness to the sinking of the city. Half of the city's water is drawn from wells with the result that over the past few decades the city is several inches lower. The monument's foundations, however, go down to bedrock to prevent it from sinking.

Independence Column stands as the main monument of Reforma Avenue.

A military parade on Reforma Avenue for Independence Day. The march begins at the Independence Column and continues on to the Zócalo, where the Military presents arms to the President. This festivity begins with the traditional "Grito" or "Yell" celebrated on the eve of the independence, commemorating the great patriot Miguel Hidalgo, who rose up in arms against the Spanish Government on September 16, 1910.

In the Art Garden, near the intersection of Reforma and Insurgentes Avenues, the Monument to the Mother stands out as an example of public projects carried out by the post-revolutionary regime. Its concave form and esplanade make it the ideal setting for popular concerts and events.

Opposite: Reforma Avenue seen towards the east; in the foreground, the circular fountain of the statue of Diana the Huntress, by architect Vicente Mendiola and sculptor Juan Francisco Olabuibel. Because of roadwork, this is the third site occupied by this fountain since 1942, when the nude statue provoked a scandal: a skirt was added, removed in 1967. In the left background, the Guadalupe Mountains.

The World Trade Center of Mexico City occupies a structure originally built as a hotel and redesigned as a center of commerce and exhibits by architect Bosco Cortina, in the early 1990s. In the southeast of the city in the left background, dramatically illuminated, is the Cerro de la Estrella hill near Iztapalapa, a town dating from pre-Hispanic times.

Opposite: The Periférico divides the Polanco district (left) from Lomas de Chapultepec (right). In the lower left is the National Conservatory by architect Mario Pani and built in the late 1950s. At center the National Auditorium stands out in the green expanse of Chapultepec Forest.

The characteristic ellipitical design of the Condesa district is due to the previous existence of a racetrack here. It is one of the first urban developments of the 20th century, as seen in the first houses from the 1920s (at left). This area is characterized not only by excellent modern architecture, but also by its green areas distributed in wide walkways and two parks. The España Park is shaped like a half moon at the center of this elliptical design, and the Park Mexico is in the smaller circle. The art deco Lindberg Theater, with its horseshoe form, completes this concentric urban space.

Another view of the Torre Mayor. To its left is the Chapultepec Castle, the monument to the Niños Héroes and the Museum of Modern Art, one of the most visited sites in Mexico City.

Opposite: In the foreground is the Torre Mayor; at center, in the middle of the forest, is the monument to the Heroic Boys and the Chapultepec Castle. This view shows the size of the Chapultepec Forest, one of the most important "green lungs" of the City.

CHAPULTEPEC AND POLANCO

Chapultepec Park with its many monuments dates from pre-Hispanic times. At its center is Chapultepec Castle, built as a fortress and remodeled by the Hapsburg Maximilian in the manner of European palaces. It has borne witness to the passage of time from its natural cliff, seen here in the 1920s when most of the Condesa district (background) was built. This landmark was used as the presidential residence until 1936, when President Lázaro Cárdenas moved to the nearby residence Los Pinos. The castle was later transformed into the National History Museum. The white semicircle (left) is dedicated to the Boy Heroes, students of the military academy who defended the castle and died during the American invasion of 1848. In the foreground is the Modern Art Museum, built in the late 1960s, designed by architect Pedro Ramirez Vázquez.

At the center of this panoramic view of Chapultepec Forest is Los Pinos, the official residence of the president. The Periférico freeway divides the original section of the forest. The amusement park La Feria (right) with its large wooden rollercoaster, the Technological Museum, and the Children's Museum together create a hub of entertainment in this newer section, developed in the 1960s.

At left, the Polanco area with its high-rise hotels towards Reforma Avenue, near Chapultepec Park, was planned initially as a residential area, but has become a fashionable district in recent years, with some of the most prestigious nightclubs in the city. Behind the hotels, inside the park, is the National Auditorium (right), built in the early 1960s and designed by architect Pedro Ramirez Vázquez. It was remodeled in the early 1990s by Teodoro González de León, to reflect the image of prosperity inspired by the presidency of Carlos Salinas de Gortari in the years NAFTA was taking shape. In the background, Campo Marte (Mars Field), used for parades and as a polo field, is crowned by an enormous flagpole.

These twin towers designed by world renowned architect Cesar Pelli stand as a landmark in the congested northern border of Chapultepec Park. The National Museum of Anthropology, by architects Pedro Ramirez Vázquez and Rafael Mijares, is easily recognizable in the green expanse of park (left) by its distinctive patio, covered by an umbrella.

To the north of Chapultepec Forest, the Periférico freeway divides two fashionable urban districts: Polanco and Las Lomas. Many high-rises have been built along this artery because they are exempt from recent restrictions on property development in both neighborhoods. In the foreground, two insurance companies flank the foundation of a future tower. In the left background, the second section of the forest marks the limit of this luxurious residential neighborhood where, as can be seen, green areas abound.

Opposite: The delicate church of San Ignacio de Loyola (lower foreground), designed in the 1960s by architect Juan Sordo Madaleno, contrasts with the monumental 1990s' Bailleres complex, by the architect's son. This commercial complex includes the Palacio de Hierro department store and an office tower.

In the heart of Polanco, the Church of San Agustín, which dates from the turn of the 20th century, is a unique concrete structure with Roman elements.

Two examples of buildings devoted to education, following classical schemes of architecture: towards Tacuba, the old Heroic Military Academy, built in the late 19th century, in a clearly French style; and the School of National Defense. Today, the city extends beyond what were then city limits into the mountains seen in the background.

At the eastern end of Lincoln Park in Polanco, the Angela Peralta Amphitheater is an ideal setting for open air concerts.

Opposite: In the newer section of Chapultepec Forest is the National Natural History Museum of the late 1960s by architect Pedro Ramírez Vázquez. At left, one of the artificial lakes within the forest.

SOUTH

In this panoramic view from the fifties, Insurgentes Avenue stands out in the foreground near Mixcoac, which until the early 20th century was a town far from the city. Its principal activity, owing to the composition of its soil, was brick manufacturing. More than one hundred years of excavation has left depressions in the land, and these later formed the foundations for the three large spaces seen here: the Mexico Bull Ring, the Blue Stadium and the Sunken Park. Bleachers are below street level in the first two, and the park is curiously isolated from urban bustle.

Four views of Insurgentes Avenue in the south part of the city. The offices of some of the most important corporations are concentrated along this artery, as well as numerous businesses and restaurants. Over the past thirty years, these buildings have substituted the homes that originally flanked this important avenue, radically changing the physical appearance of the residential zones developed here during the fifties and sixties.

Opposite: The intersection of Insurgentes, Chapultepec and Oaxaca avenues, at the Insurgentes roundabout and subway station. With the "Zona Rosa" and neighborhoods such as Juárez, Roma and Condesa nearby, this is a popular meeting point in the city. Insurgentes Avenue is one of the longest streets in the world at nearly 30 kilometers, with distinctive tall buildings to the south.

The tradition of bullfighting is considered by some a carnage, by others a religious ritual to complete every Sunday during the season. The Mexico Bull Ring is the landmark of this celebration, attracting well known stars and politicians.

Opposite: The intersection of Cuauhtémoc, Universidad and División del Norte Avenues, in the Del Valle district, is known as the Riviera turnabout. The pedestrian bridge is the only circular remnant of the old turnabout, which disappeared after roadwork in the sixties. At right, the church of the Miraculous Medal, a pleated structure, was built in the late fifties, designed by architect Félix Candela—one of the most important architects of the 20th century in the use of light structures made of concrete.

Coyoacán, a pre-Hispanic urban center transformed at the beginning of the sixteenth century into a colonial town, remains as a picturesque enclave, surrounded by 1950s urban developments. The main plaza (right) is the former atrium of a religious complex, torn down during the War of Reform in the nineteenth century.

University City houses the main campus of the National Autonomous University of Mexico (UNAM). Designed by the leading architects of the time, led by Enrique del Moral and Mario Pani, the campus was erected in the late 1950s as part of the modernization endorsed by president Miguel Alemán. As viewed in the background, right, the Olympic Stadium (left) forms a gentle silhouette against the mountains towards the western boundary of the campus.

The University's Rectory Tower and Central Library (left) with the plazas between them, are examples of how the tradition of pre-Hispanic urbanism was blended with modern movements of the twentieth century. In the southern limits of the campus, the university maintains a natural preserve in which modern sculptures have been erected against volcanic lava (right). The complex was designed by Mathias Goeritz, Helen Escobedo, Manuel Felguerez, Sebastian and Herzua.

In the background to the southeast of the city is the town of Iztapalapa, a pre-Hispanic settlement at the foot of the Cerro de la Estrella hill. In the foreground, the Tlalpan area can be distinguished by its dense foliage. Nearby, the Aztec Stadium (right), built for the World Soccer Cup in 1970 and designed by the architects Pedro Ramírez Vázquez and Rafael Mijares, is among the largest stadiums of the world, with a capacity of nearly 100,000 spectators.

Opposite: To the south of the valley is Xochimilco, the last trace of the pre-Hispanic system of floating gardens and canals dedicated to intensive agriculture. The main church (left), in the central garden, is the heart of an urban design, partially surrounded by a vast system of bodies of water, seen in the foreground. In the left background, the Guadalupe Mountains, and to the right, the Texcoco Lake Basin.

On the edge of the canals of Xochimilco, where tourists and locals spend outings on picturesque boats, are the ahuejotes. These trees are planted on the edge of the chinampas, or floating gardens, to help compact the earth of these artificial islands, dedicated to intensive agriculture. The ahuejotes, with their spiky silhouettes, contribute to the bucolic character of this ancestral landscape.

To the south near Tlalpan, the México golf club stands outs as a large green expanse, with the Aztec Stadium in the background. The circular pyramid of the archaeological zone of Cuicuilco (right) is the last vestige of one of the oldest settlements in the valley. This urban complex, which dates from about 800 BC, established a commercial and cultural hegemony in the Valley of Mexico in the 5th century BC. A direct historical antecedent of Teotihuacan, this center was brutally destroyed by a lava eruption from the Xitle volcano in the first century BC.

The Campestre Golf Club (left) contrasts sharply with the compact urban area near Coyoacán. Founded in the late 19th century by the English community, it was the first golf course in all of Mexico. On the north side, distinguished by its characteristic architectural forms, is the National Center of the Arts (right), built in the early nineties to project a vision of modernization and economic rebirth.

In the volcanic range to the south of the city, the Heroic Military Academy of the 1970s stands out for its precise geometry. Designed by architect Agustín Hernández, it is perhaps not an accurate interpretation of formal pre-Hispanic language, yet it is a monumental integration of pre-Columbian architecture with modern urban design.

Opposite: The tilled hills of Milpa Alta, to the extreme southeast of the valley, are a vestige of previously intensive agricultural activity in this area, with the volcanoes Ixtaccihuatl and Popocatépetl in the background.

EAST

Since the late seventies, considerable expanses of pastureland have been successfully cultivated with water from Texcoco Lake (right). This measure has almost completely eliminated the whirling dust that previously covered the city every year around February, from the dry exposed earth and intense winter winds.

Opposite: In this panoramic view from the east we can observe how the Benito Juárez airport has been devoured by the growth of the city, making its relocation an imperative. At center right, the irregular green patch is the Rodríguez Brothers Race Track, and to the left of the airport, the Aragón Forest. In the background, what remains of Texcoco Lake; at right, the Nabor Carrillo Lake, a vestige of a lake that previously covered almost the entire valley.

The outskirts of the city are clear in the basin
of what was once Lake Texcoco, the backyard
of the city. At left, one of the main city
dumps, in the municipality of Nezahualcóyotl,
and in the background, the airport. At right,
the Eastside Prison, in the same municipality.

To the east of the city, near the airport, one can see patterns of urban experimentation from the twenties and thirties. At left, in an octagonal design, is the Federal neighborhood. Opposite, Africa Plaza is the starting point of several diagonal streets that weave together the Romero Rubio neighborhood. Upper left is the airport.

Above left: The eastern bus station, TAPO, along with the Congress (at center), stand out as the most important structures to the east of the historic district (background). The station was built in the seventies and designed by architect Juan Díaz Infante.

Above right: The General Archive of the Nation (right), to the southeast of the historic district, is at the site of the previous Lecumberri prison. Its radial pattern is a typical example of early 19th century prison architecture.

Opposite: The Congress (left) holds the lower house, built in the late 1970s, to the east of the historic district. Designed by architect Pedro Ramírez Vázquez, this project took shape in the policy of 'openness' and increased representation of the people, begun during José López Portillo's presidency.

The city had its first encounter with aviation at the Balbuena airdrome only a few miles from the current airport (left). The same area (right), completely urbanized, here in a panoramic view towards the north, with the Guadalupe mountain range upper left.

In this view of the south of the city, looking east, the Pedro Enriquez Ureña Avenue or Eje 10 Sur can be seen at center. This avenue separates the Pedregal de San Francisco neighborhood, at left, from the Pedregal de Santo Domingo, at right. In the difference between trees and density, on each side, the contrast is clear between the two communities.

Opposite: The Mormon Temple of the 1980s is in an apparent Neo-Mayan style. In the green mass in the background, the Aragon forest stands out as a point of contrast within urban sameness, characteristic of the eastern part of the city (right).

WEST

Only a few years ago, the city ended and the highway to Toluca began at the foot of the buildings to the right, where Reforma and Constituyentes Avenues converge. Since the late eighties, the city has overflowed into the western hills with widespread urban construction: residential, commercial and financial, developments alternating between ravines. Upper left, is the National Park, Desierto de los Leones. In the background, the Nevado de Toluca volcano.

In the hills to the west of the valley are luxurious residential, commercial and financial developments, between golf courses, competing with low-income settlements with high density and few public services. At left, the urban development of Santa Fe is one of the city's most recent, settled on top of old sand mines.

Two views from the same angle, but at different altitudes, of the Interlomas Golf Course. This is one of the most ambitious developments in the western hills of the city, and includes residential buildings and one-family houses within its perimeters. In the background, in both images, against characteristic morning fog, is the immutable sillhouette of the volcanoes Iztaccíhuatl and Popocatépetl. At right, in the background, the highway to Toluca passes through Santa Fe cooperative developments.

In Santa Fe and Interlomas, high-rise residential buildings are chaotically mixed with one-family homes. In the background, the Tepehuatzin mountains separate the Valley of Mexico from the Valley of Toluca.

Opposite: Corporate and residential buildings strung along a ravine take the shape of a fish in this development of Bosques de las Lomas.

Among the most ambitious developments in the western hills of the city is the Interlomas Golf Club, which includes housing developments in its perimeter. Known as "The Pants," this corporate development, built in the mid nineties and designed by architect Teodoro González de León, constitutes an inevitable urban landmark that is elegant to some and without character to others.

94

In the western hills it is not uncommon to find this kind of space, where luxurious residential, commercial and business areas compete with high-density development.

Opposite: At sunset, the Altus Tower of the early nineties, by architect Augusto Álvarez, is distinguished from the buildings around it by its airiness and slender figure. In the left background, a different view of the Popocatépetl volcano.

Towards the Interlomas zone, the outline of the high buildings on Paseo de la Reforma is clear.

Opposite: A sequence of hills and ravines in the west of the city looking south: Interlomas, Santa Fe, Las Águilas and Contreras. In the background are the Ajusco mountains.

In the west of the city, educational centers of all different levels have proliferated among new housing developments.

Opposite: Here is the more modern of the two branches of the nationally vital Ángeles Hospital.

Pre-Hispanic designs leap out in the pavement of the West Alameda Park.

Opposite: The Coronado building appears as a cube in the inscribed circles of architect Agustín Hernández. At right, the brick buildings of the prestigious Jesuit Iberoamericana University, by architect Francisco Serrano.

NORTH

The design of the atrium of the Basílica de Guadalupe is clear in this 1968 photograph, at left, dominated by the old temple of the late 17th century. Crowding and structural considerations made a new church necessary in the seventies (right). Architect Pedro Ramírez Vázquez created this controversial reconstruction.

On this exact site, the Virgin of Guadalupe is believed to have appeared to Juan Diego and asked him to build a temple in her honor. This place is frequented as much as the Basilica, where her image can be found, miraculously fixed on Juan Diego's ayate (sarape made of natural fibers).

Opposite: The Old Basílica de Guadalupe is the destination of many Catholic pilgrimages from all over the Americas. This sanctuary, devoted to the Virgin of Guadalupe, stands at the foot of a sacred mountain (upper right), devoted to the pre-Hispanic goddess Tonantzin.

At the intersection of Insurgentes Avenue and the Circuito Interior is the Monument to La Raza, a contribution to nationalist spirit. It was conceived, paradoxically, not as a fusion of colonial and pre-Hispanic forms, but as a deliberate caricature of a pre-Hispanic pyramid. It is crowned by an eagle that is more imperial than republican.

Opposite: The triangular outline of the Banobras Tower in Tlatelolco stands out to the north on Insurgentes Avenue. Built in the fifties and designed by architect Mario Pani, its form is shaped by a very efficient principle of structural triangulation, which is exposed in the upper levels. In the center background is the Torre Mayor, and at right the Pemex tower.

To the north on the highway to Querétaro, amidst a landscape of shopping malls and housing developments, the 1950s Satélite Towers stands out as an urban milestone. They were designed by architect Luis Barragán and artist Mathias Goeritz. The name originates from their pioneering effort.

Between Polanco and Tacuba during the early 20th century, the breweries of Cervecería Modelo were dominant industrial forces.

111

In these two images of the foothills in the north of the valley is a colonial aqueduct at left, and at right a cemetery on the top of a hill.

The municipality of Atizapán is hemmed in between forested hills in the southwest end of the valley among golf course developments, such as Chiluca and Britannia.

Covering 52 hectares, the new Racetrack of the Americas is one of a kind. The architecture of the new installations was developed following a concept of functional excellence and high technology, which puts it in the category of the best racetracks in the world. In the second stage of the complex, a Center of Cultural Training was built, with a Mexican plaza and a multipurpose arena, where the best charrería (Mexican rodeo) events are held. This sports center also includes a Modern Convention Center and an ample space for exhibits.

Opposite: The charreada, is a spectacle close to the activity of the ranches and former haciendas, still popular in the large cities, as in this charro arena in the middle of the city.

117

TEOTIHUACÁN

Northeast of the city center are the remains of the majestic city of Teotihuacán. The Pyramid of the Sun stands out in the foreground, and behind it the Pyramid of the Moon. When the Aztecs arrived at the Valley of Mexico in the 14th century, this city had already been abandoned. Here are hidden some of the oldest mysteries of ancient Mexico.

Teotihuacán was the first major pre-Hispanic urban complex (circa 300 BC– 600 AD), on the outskirts of what was once the lake of México, now densely populated by urban development. At right, in the foreground, presiding over the Calzada de los Muertos (Avenue of the Dead), is the Pyramid of the Moon, and to the left is the Pyramid of the Sun. In the right background, the rapid growth of the northeast urban area impinges on this archaeological complex, declared a heritage of mankind by UNESCO.

Presiding over the Avenue of the Dead in Teotihuacán is the Pyramid of the Moon. In pre-Hispanic cities the most important monuments were devoted to the deities of the sky, and therefore were strategically arranged according to astronomical considerations. On top of the pyramids, on the *teocalli*, the priests carried out sacred ceremonies, which could include human sacrifices.

On the south end of Teotihuacán is the Palace of Quetzalcóatl, which appears here in the foreground. The Avenue of the Dead, visible in the background at left, is the street joining this ceremonial complex. In the background is the Pyramid of the Sun.

Opposite: Inscriptions made with stone and lime, and a flag on a mountain near Teotihuacán. This photograph shows part of the Santa Lucía military training camp. This landmark is between the Zumpango and Xaltocan lakes in the northeast of Mexico City.

PUEBLA, CHOLULA, TLAXCALA AND VICINITY

The great pyramid of Cholula, over the remains of which a church was built, was constructed at the dawn of this city's splendor, around the year 700 A.D. The size of its base indicates that it was one of the largest pyramids erected in the pre-Hispanic world. Although this city continued to be inhabited at the time of the arrival of Hernán Cortez in 1519, its power and splendor had ended during the 9th century. In the background is the city of Puebla, 10 kilometers east.

East of the valley, on the other side of the Nevada mountains, is the city of Cholula. This settlement from pre-Hispanic times is virtually a suburb of Puebla. (Left) At center is the main plaza of Cholula. At left center is the atrium of the main church, and above is the great pre-Hispanic pyramid crowned by a colonial church, as a symbol of the cultural subjugation of the conquest. (Right) A general panorama with the pyramid in the foreground and the Nevada mountains (not very snowy in this image) in the background, with the Popocatépetl and Iztaccihuatl volcanoes seen from an inverted perspective to the view from Mexico City.

The historical center of the city of Puebla, 76 miles east of Mexico City, is characterized by its ornate colonial architecture, among which several churches and convents stand out, as seen in the image to the left. The cathedral (right), positioned to one side of the main plaza, is another marvel for which this city is well known. Since its foundation in the 16th century, the city of Puebla became a point of junction between Mexico City and the port of Veracruz on the Gulf of Mexico.

On the outskirts of the city of Puebla is the Volkswagen factory, one of the largest complexes of this automobile company.

Opposite: The strategic position of Puebla since the 19th century has made it an important hub of industrial development. Urbanization of large expanses of territory followed. Here a park area has been preserved around an ancient aqueduct.

Ancient, formerly agricultural communities mix in a network of commerce between Puebla, Texmelucan, Tlaxcala and Apizaco. Around the church and main plaza of a typical town, one can see the resulting improvisation and irregularity.

To the north of the city of Tlaxcala, this town at left exemplifies the contrast common in many communities between the colonial center and recent indiscriminate development.

At right, the Sanctuary of the Virgin of Ocotlán, near the city of Tlaxcala, is a jewel of the Mexican baroque. Built in the 17th century, this church is known for the dynamism between the upper body of its towers and the central facade, achieved by brick layover on the lower body of the towers.

Structures dating from the Colonial period
in the southeast of the valley: Right, a
hacienda characteristic of the 19th century.
Left, a cemetery outside a small town in the
monumental style of popular funeral architecture in Mexico.

133

Large expanses of land are cultivated for grain in the state of Tlaxcala, to the southeast of Mexico City. Here a humble country structure, built in stone, contrasts with the typical idea of a new "Mexican" ranch.

Opposite: Here a town has developed around the remains of an ancient colonial church. An unfinished nave, the tombs of a small cemetery…

Here the ruins of an old hacienda crossed by a road. Among several standing structures are a chapel and several cloisters around a succession of patios. During the Revolution of 1910 some haciendas were abandoned or plundered by troops from both sides and many were never inhabited again.

With terraces to channel water, here at the foot of the Nevada mountains abundant springs support intensive agriculture. Straight rows give way to concentric circles around a hill. This agricultural region stretches from the east of Hidalgo state to the state of Tlaxcala.

From the northeastern side of the mountain range separating the valley of Mexico from Puebla, the volcanoes Iztaccíhuatl in the foreground and Popocatépetl in the background are visible. This angle is reminiscent of some of the famous paintings created by José María Velasco in the late 19th century. At right a mountain range shows how agriculture has taken over the woodlands. In the left background, between clouds, are Pico de Orizaba, the highest volcano in North America, and to its right, La Malinche.

At left the northeast side of Iztaccíhuatl, at right, the Popocatépetl crater. According to pre-Hispanic legend, Iztaccíhuatl is "the sleeping woman" in a spell, identified by her silhouette, and Popocatépetl is the masculine sentinel who watches over her, waiting for her to awake.

OUTSIDE THE CITY

The Tequesquitengo (right) and Valle de Bravo reservoirs are two of the most popular weekend destinations for inhabitants of the "great city," as natural lakes are scarce. Sixty-eight miles south of the capital in Morelos state, Tequesquitengo has a pleasant climate all year round. On its shore are some luxurious developments as well as piers and swimming pools. Here aquatic sports include diving down to a church submerged in the water. The colonial town of Valle de Bravo (left) is 75 miles to the west of the city in Mexico state, in a forested zone in the Nevado de Toluca mountains. The moderate winds that regularly comb this valley make it the ideal site for sailing and hang-gliding. In the left foreground, the colonial center with the main plaza and church. In the background, developments that have somewhat conserved the density of the forest.

At a distance of 55 miles to the south of Mexico City, the city of Cuernavaca, with a generous climate at an altitude of less than a mile, is a favorite vacation spot. Spanish conqueror Hernán Cortés established one of his residences here. The church at left, in Neo-Gothic style, was built in concrete at the turn of the 20th century.

At right, typical weekend vacation homes with swimming pool, gardens and, in some, a tennis court.

Opposite: The 'city of the never ending spring' is home to a cathedral crowning the center of the city (right), with a large atrium and open chapel dating from the 16th century. The exuberant vegetation surrounding it in parks and gardens gives this tourist destination its sobriquet.

147

The Archaeological Zone of Teopanzolco, within the urban area of Cuernavaca, with the Tepozteco hills (left) in the background. In the process of restoration here (right), several different construction stages can be seen in the layering of structures on pre-Hispanic architecture.

Twenty kilometers to the southwest of Cuernavaca is the archaeological zone of Xochicalco. During its prime, this civilization achieved hegemony in the south of the Valley of Mexico, between the fall of Teotihuacán (circa 650 AD) and the consolidation of Tula (circa 900 AD). This fortified urban center demonstrates the magnificent symbiotic relationship between pre-Hispanic civilization and mountainous terrain.

Forty-three miles to the southwest of the valley is the town of Tenango de Arista and nearby, the archaeological zone of Teotenango. These images are unique in the way they illustrate many climates of the Central Mexican Plateau. In geological terms, there is a system of primitive mountain ranges, superimposed by the recent eruption of lava from a volcano belonging to the neo-volcanic range (lower right in both images) upon which the pre-Hispanic city was settled. The wild vegetation contrasts between coniferous forests on soft soil and scrub on volcanic rock. Much more recently, the first human intervention was the ceremonial pre-Hispanic complex, with terraces and pavilions built by extraction and addition of the same volcanic mass. At the foot of this complex, on soft soil, a minor village with agricultural land was wiped out in the 16th century by the colonial center and an increase in agricultural activity. Recently, logging almost to the top of the surrounding peaks and urban and industrial sprawl have changed the landscape, Teotenango was one of the city states, like Xochicalco, developed between the fall of Teotihuacán, around 650 A.D., and the consolidation of Tula, around 850 A.D.

On the left, the Lascurián hacienda used for the production of pulque, and on the right another 19th century hacienda in the state of Hildago.

The archaeological zone of Tula was the political, military and religious center of the Toltec culture. It arose 200 years after the fall of Teotihuacan, the dominant culture of the Central Mexican Plateau. Its splendor lasted more than three hundred years, from the mid 9th to the mid 12th century, when Chichimec migrations from the north intensified. On top of the largest pyramid are the famous Atlantes, which represent deities, seen as columns. In the foreground, the complex known as the Group of One Thousand Columns.

Opposite: To the north of the city, near Tula, waste water is treated in the Endo reservoir, before following its course east to the Gulf of Mexico. In the foreground, a chapel remains half covered by the water. Humidity and the concentration of organic material has turned these dry regions into wetlands.

157

Nevado de Toluca National Park (left), to the west of the city of Toluca, has large expanses of woods for camping. The main attraction in this park is the Nevado de Toluca volcano, at 4,690 meters above sea level. In its crater, accessed by car on a winding road, are two lagoons.